T0137511

A Poetic Invitation
Volume 2

# Are You Looking for Love?

*The Love of God Is Looking for You*

## Faye Stewart

WESTBOW
PRESS®
A DIVISION OF THOMAS NELSON
& ZONDERVAN

This book is a work of non-fiction. Unless otherwise noted, the author and the publisher make no explicit guarantees as to the accuracy of the information contained in this book and in some cases, names of people and places have been altered to protect their privacy.

WestBow Press books may be ordered through booksellers or by contacting:

WestBow Press
A Division of Thomas Nelson & Zondervan
1663 Liberty Drive
Bloomington, IN 47403
www.westbowpress.com
1 (866) 928-1240

Because of the dynamic nature of the Internet, any web addresses or links contained in this book may have changed since publication and may no longer be valid. The views expressed in this work are solely those of the author and do not necessarily reflect the views of the publisher, and the publisher hereby disclaims any responsibility for them.

Any people depicted in stock imagery provided by Getty Images are models, and such images are being used for illustrative purposes only. Certain stock imagery © Getty Images.

Scripture taken from the King James Version of the Bible.

ISBN: 978-1-9736-7928-8 (sc)
ISBN: 978-1-9736-7929-5 (e)

Library of Congress Control Number: 2019917988

Print information available on the last page.

WestBow Press rev. date: 01/30/2020

## Dedications

To my "3 TXSONS"—Steven, Mike, and Paul—and three adored grandchildren—Robert, Kaitlyn, and Bryan—You keep my heart smiling!

To my devoted sister, Evelyn—Thank you for your steadfast support of all my endeavors throughout life!

To my special cousin Dale who always stirs my heart to "press on!"—You are my example of complete devotion to Christ.

To my wonderful friends in Virginia and Texas—Thank you for your love, support, and prayers that avail much!

In conclusion, to my precious mom who always encouraged me in my writing.

# Contents

Acknowledgments ....................................................... ix

Introduction ............................................................. xi

1   Names of God................................................ 1
2   Creation ...................................................... 9
3   Grace.......................................................... 15
4   Faith/Believe ............................................... 23
5   The Cross.................................................... 29
6   Commitment................................................ 45
7   Relationship................................................. 49
8   People ........................................................ 67
9   Heaven ....................................................... 77
10 Funerals ..................................................... 89
11 Witnessing .................................................. 95

Benediction............................................................. 105

About the Author ................................................... 107

# Acknowledgments

To my Lord and Savior Jesus Christ who makes all things possible.

With appreciation also to the WestBow Press team in transitioning these poems from my heart to the printed page. Your leadership has made this journey a satisfying one.

# Introduction

God has been looking for us since the garden of Eden. We prefer to go our own way.

The plan of salvation was ordained before the beginning of the world. God sent his only Son, Jesus, to bear the sins of the world on Calvary. The shame and pain that he willingly bore on our behalf hovered over the cross. But so did love.

And that love is still looking for "whosoever will" to come to him (John 3:16). In your personal search for love, try beginning at the cross. "Greater love hath no man than this, that a man lay down his life" (John 15:13).

Christ died for you. Will you consider living for him?

# *1*

# Names of God

---

## God Knows Your Name    (Isaiah 43:1)

There is a God in heaven,
And he knows your name.
You're the reason he came to earth,
That you may know your worth to him.

---

## The One Who Rules Eternity  (Isaiah 57:15a)

Eternity—
The place where God dwells
And rules in majesty over all.
His power, presence, and sovereignty
Are the same as before the fall.

Who but God can walk on the wings of the wind
Or part waters of a sea?
Make countless snowflakes none alike?
Breathe breath into you and me?

Eternity—
So far away, yet so near.
Years without number fill the universe,
And all the while he is here!

## Ancient of Days  (Daniel 7:9)

Glorious, how glorious is your name!
How perfect are your ways.
Now and forever, you are always the same.
I pledge thee my troth, O Ancient of Days.

## Salvation Was Born (Luke 2:11–12)

God became flesh—
Victory in a manger!

## Jesus, the Highest of Gifts   (John 1:12)


Jesus,
The highest of gifts
To common men.

His love from the cross
Can transform us into heavenly kin.

## One of Us   (Philippians 2:7)

You came to earth as a babe.
On the cross your life you gave.
You rose triumphant from the grave.

You lived your life as one of us.
And all the while,
You were *God*.

## Life (John 14:6)

At the beginning of your earthly journey,
Your home was Mary's womb.   (Luke 2:4-5)

After your death on a cruel cross,
Your brief home was a tomb.   (Luke 23:50-53)

Mary's womb, a garden tomb—   (Luke 2:6-7; Matthew 28:5-9)
Each gave birth to life!

# 2

# Creation

---

**Spring Snow**   (Isaiah 55:10)

As I sit in my rocking chair,
Looking out my window,
I watch the snowfall.
Soft, silent, white—
To my eyes, a delight.

It is a morning gift from our Creator.
And the funniest thing,
It's the second day of spring!

---

## Oh, the Beauty of a Foggy Morn (Revelation 22:20)

Oh, the beauty of an early morning fog
With the sun as large as a harvest moon
Softly visible behind it.

The bright mist-covered light
Beckons my spirit to rise
And meet him in the air.
My heart takes flight!

The sun as large as a harvest moon
Could be a sign that he's coming soon!

## The Morning Light Danced (Ecclesiastes 11:7)


I viewed the full morning sun,
Beyond bright in its glow.

Its rays from heaven touched
The bay water's gentle flow.

As far as you could see,
Light danced in rhythm
On the soft waves below.

Yet another God moment
That thrilled my heart so!

# Spring Sprung!   (Song of Solomon 2:12)

I was on my way from the house to the car.
It was bright and sunny.
The birds were in full chorus singing
While it was "springing."

Even little birds know
And share the fun
Of a spring day in December
Gifted by the Son.

It reminds me of God's creativity
During this season of Christ's nativity.
No one but God could devise such a plan—
A babe in a manger, redemption for man.

Thank you, Lord Jesus,
For salvation you bring!
New life with you
Becomes forever spring.

## Raining Leaves (John 3:8a)

I love it when it rains leaves!
Branches briskly bend,
And fall colors blend
As the leaves descend,
Floating to the end
Of their ride.

They go where the wind blows them.
No struggle, free flight.
What a sight!
Oh, how I love it when it rains leaves!

# *3*

# Grace

---

## And Yet (Romans 5:8)

Worthy I am not.
And yet,
You died for me!

---

## How Must You Have Felt (Genesis 2:7)

Father God,
How must you have felt
When you perhaps knelt
To breathe life into your own Son?

From heaven to earth,
At our Savior's birth
Came love from heaven above.

## Unexpected Grace   (Ephesians 1:7)

Don't you love that wonderful place
Of unexpected grace?

Grace from the cross—
Always seeking the lost—
Reaches down from above
Pouring out in red, love.

"Come unto me all who will.
Your life I'll change.
Your heart I'll fill.

Say yes to my plea
And walk with me
From the foot of the cross
Into eternity."

## Grace and Love (Ephesians 3:19)

Your grace,
Indescribable.

Your love,
Undeniable.

Grace and love sent from above
Alight on our hearts like a dove.

## He Regarded Our Low Estate     (Psalm 136:23)

Tasting death through God's grace,
Christ regarded our low estate.
His love spent on our behalf
Conquered sin, every trace!

## Heirs of Grace (Romans 8:16-17)

Grace flows through our veins.
Heirs of grace are we.
From Christ it pours into our hearts
With love from Calvary.

## Amazing, Your Grace (Psalm 45:2a)

The more I view the cross
Fairer becomes your face.
Amazing, the love.
Amazing, your grace.

# 4

# Faith/Believe

---

**You Are Faithful**   (Revelation 19:11)

From the dawning of the day
To the setting of the sun,
You are faithful.

---

## He Remains
## Faithful   (Deuteronomy 7:9; 2 Timothy 2:13)

When I stumble and fall,
He remains faithful.

When I refuse his call,
He remains faithful.

When I build in my heart a wall,
He remains faithful.

What kind of love is this?
Love beyond compare.
He who cannot deny himself
Will always be there.

He promised!

## I Believe You Prayed for Me  (Mark 14:35–36)

Lord Jesus,

I believe you prayed for me
In Gethsemane.

## I Believe You Died for Me   (John 3:16)

Lord Jesus,

I believe you died for me
At Calvary.

## He Is Always There for Me   (Jeremiah 31:3)

Whenever I call,
Whatever my plea,
He who drew me to the cross
Is always there for me.

## Believe on the Lord Jesus Christ   (Acts 16:31)

What are you holding on to?
Your works?
It may all be for naught.
Your money?
By its many cares, your soul is caught.
Your position in life,
Does it make you proud?
Your voice of influence?
You sure can draw the crowds.

What will you hold on to
When life is close to o'er?
Will your works, money, position, and voice
See you safely through death's door?

What was that saying I once heard?
"For we brought nothing into this world,
And it is certain we will carry nothing out."

Dear Lord, how can I safely get through that door
Without suffering loss?
Believe on the Lord Jesus Christ,
And hold on, hold on to the cross!

# 5

# The Cross

---

## Salvation

### Infinite Love (John 3:16)

You stepped from eternity into time
That we might step from time into eternity,
And be with you.

Oh, the infinite love of God!

---

## Gethsemane (Hebrews 12:2)


Such intimacy in Gethsemane,
A settled peace that came with obedience,
Even in the face of Calvary.

The cross was endured
Because the joy set before you was settled in prayer,
In Gethsemane.

## Look unto Jesus (Luke 10:39–42)

Be still my heart.
Let go earthly quests.
Why settle for less
When you can have the best?

Look unto Jesus,
The Lamb that was slain.
You have nothing to lose
And everything to gain!

## Where Would I Be? (Colossians 2:13–14)

Where would I be for eternity
If my sins weren't nailed to Calvary's tree?

## Paid in Full  (1 Peter 1:18-19)

Paid in full—
Oh, the thought.

From sin's curse
I have been bought!

## "Come unto Me"  (Matthew 11:28)

While walking through my house one day, I paused.
I heard a voice, a lovely voice I'd never heard before.

"Come unto me and I will give you rest."
These words made my heart rise, much to my surprise.

With newborn hope, I accepted his invitation
And was filled with peace beyond imagination.

Amazing grace, how sweet the sound
That filled my heart with love profound.

## Redeeming Love (Isaiah 43:1)

Redeeming love has called my name
And I will never be the same!

# The Blood

## You Stayed  (John 15:13a)

You stayed
Until every drop of blood was spilled.
What kind of love is this
That stayed on the cross?

Lord, never let the memory fade
Of your love and the blood you shed
The day you stayed on the cross,
For me.

**Are You Looking for Love?**   (Proverbs 8:17)

Are you looking for love?
Look at the cross.
The love of God is looking for *you*.

## What Is Love? (John 3:16)

What is love?
A crown made of thorns,
A whip made with pieces of glass and rock,
Nails hammered into flesh,
A thrusting sword,
A rugged tree to hang on until the last drop of blood
and the last breath were spent for "whosoever will."

## Lamb of Calvary   (Isaiah 45:22)

O Lamb of Calvary,
As I gaze upon the tree
And see you dying there for me,
All I can do is take in the view, silently.

## Love Beyond Degree   (Luke 23:34a; John 17:24)


What can be ascribed to thee?
Love beyond degree.

As you were led to Calvary
Then nailed to a tree
For me? Oh, no, for me.

The first words you said
While thorns pierced your head were,
"Father, forgive them,
They know not what they do."

What made you pray?
What made you stay?

You looked beyond your agony
And heard my sinner's plea;
Paying the cost while I was still lost
Just so I could be with thee.

This is love beyond degree!

## Washing Day  (Revelation 1:5)

It's washing day;
Time to wash my sins away.
All I have to do is pray,
"Precious Lord, have your way.

At your feet my sins I lay.
No more will I go astray.
Close to your cross I will stay.
Thank you, Jesus, for washing day!"

## It Snowed (Isaiah 1:18)

Thank you, Lord Jesus,
For your blood that flowed.

And thank you, thank you
For the day it snowed!

It fell so white.
Darkness turned to light.

Everything changed.
My life was rearranged
The day your love
Snowed on my heart.

## The Pearl   (Matthew 13:46)


From a heart of ice
To finding the pearl of great price!

Thank you, Lord Jesus, for dying for me.

*6*

# Commitment

---

## Life Is Short   (James 4:14)

Life is short at best.
What are you going to do
With the rest
Of yours?

---

## Now I Walk with Thee (Luke 24:13–15)

I once was lost, but now I'm found.
Was blind, but now I see.
Many were the days I ran from you,
But now I walk with thee.
How sweet to walk with thee.

## A Steadfast Heart (Proverbs 4:23a)

Oh for a love that wants to be with you,
Bringing nothing from this world
But a steadfast, quiet heart
That will transport me to your world apart.

Every day a new beginning.
Every day a new start.
Lord, help me love you with a steadfast heart.

## Intertwined (Ephesians 1:13–14; 2:19)

Lord Jesus,
You, the cross, and me—
Once we were three.
But when I answered your plea
To join you for eternity
Our hearts became one.
And now, new life with you has begun!

Amazing love from Calvary,
My heart is intertwined with thee.
And now I will forever be
Part of your family.

# 7

# Relationship

---

## Earthen Vessel  (2 Corinthians 4:7)

Earthen vessel though I be,
God's Spirit lives inside me.

Working through this pot of clay
With perfect love,
Lord, have your way.

---

## Rent the Veil (Matthew 27:51a)

Rent the veil of my heart, Lord,
Top to bottom, heaven to earth.

Keep me by the sword of the Spirit
That brought me second birth.

## Mercy Drops Fall Like Rain (Psalms 72:6a; 100:5a)

Mercy drops fall like rain
On my sin-sick soul.
They wash me anew
And make me whole.

What can I say,
Lord Jesus, to thee?
Thank you for setting me
Yet again free.

May mercy drops fall
As my heart to you calls,
"Rain on, dear Jesus, rain on!"

## Draw My Heart   (Song of Solomon 1:4a)


My Lord, my God and Savior,
Ever draw my heart to thee.
May it soar to highest heaven
And grow as vast as the shining sea.

## Lord, Help Me to Remember   (James 5:7)

Lord, help me to remember
As I walk each day through,
While the wait seems long at times
You are waiting too.

## Arise and Go Forth (Proverbs 7:15)


Everywhere, everywhere,
There is nowhere he is not.

Anytime is mine to choose.
Arise, my heart, and go forth to meet him!

## In Your Presence  (Psalm 16:11b)

In your presence
I'm suspended in time,
Experiencing the eternal now.
Sublime, sublime!

## Wonder Begins Anew   (Psalm 139:13–17; 1 Thessalonians 4:15–18)

While reading familiar verses
Wonder begins anew,
Bringing thoughts of my beginning
And ending in eternity with you!

## When You Speak    (Psalm 119:130)

When you speak,
Help us to listen.

May your words
Like dewdrops glisten,
Refreshing our hearts
And bringing a new start
To each and every day
As we go our way.

## Overwhelmed (Psalm 34:4)

Overwhelmed by thoughts inside me,
Others have it far, far worse.
Even so, I painfully struggle.
Oh, Lord, how I hate the curse!

But I know you watch me from above
With eyes of love and compassion too.
You will rescue me from all my fears.
You will see me through!

## Coming Near (James 4:8a)

Thank you, Lord, for coming near.
Thank you for making my mind clear.
You are to me the dearest of the dear.

## As We Commune (Luke 24:32)

As we commune, Lord,
My heart ignites at the sound of your voice.
My mind imagines the light in your eyes.
You captivate my very soul.

## One Step Ahead   (John 10:4)

One step ahead are you, Lord,
Never far, always close.
Ever close when I reach for your hand
And hear you say, "Yes, my child, you can—

You can follow me, step by step.
I rejoice to lead the way
On your pilgrimage from earth to heaven
Day by day, by day, by day."

## Where to Begin (John 8:36)

Dear Jesus,

You freed us from the debt of sin.
How to thank you,
Where to begin.

## Nail-Scarred Hand (Isaiah 49:16)

Nail-scarred hand that holds my heart,
Never leave me, never part.

## Scenes from Calvary (Galatians 2:20)

Scenes from Calvary
Come into view
Every time I think of you,
Lord Jesus.

## Still, Small Voice     (1 Kings 19:12)

When voices around me
With distractions ring,
Your still, small voice
Can make my heart sing!

# People

---

**Happy Birthday, Mom**   (1 Thessalonians 4:16–18)

March 23—

Oh Mom how I miss you,
Especially today.
It's your birthday I'm remembering,
And you're so far away.

I know you are well and happy,
But my heart still feels that familiar tug.
While you live in God's grace and glory,
Your daughter needs a hug.

---

## Happy Birthday, My Amazing Grandkids! (Proverbs 17:6a)

"You're how many years old today?
No way—
You are growing up too fast!"
That's what grandmas always say.

Always remember you are loved
Each and every day.
You fill my heart with memories,
And there you will always stay!

## Banquets of the Soul   (John 21:12a)

(To my dear friend Evelyn, December 29, 2016)

There is nothing like dinner with a friend.
So much to share, where to begin.
First we hold hands in prayer,
And thank God for the food and his care.

While dining, we talk about the news and weather.
That soon changes to walks down memory lane.
Oh, the fun of a meal together!

Eyes open wide, they shine and twinkle
At words softly spoken.
It's worth the wrinkles!

Heart to heart, our spirits meet
When Christ joins our meal.
We pause in quiet moments,
And there his presence we feel.

Then, when we have to part
And go our separate ways,
We hug and smile because we know
These banquets of the soul
Are but a taste of heaven's endless day!

From the Bible

## The Thief on a Cross at Calvary (Luke 23:42–43)


Is it possible
That Jesus smiled once while on the cross? (my thought.)

While suffering and defeating sin
He looked at the thief and said to him,
"Today you will be with me in paradise."

## Lazarus (John 11:43–44)

I wonder what Lazarus thought
When your death on the cross was wrought.

While some wagged heads and mocked,
"Himself he cannot save,"
Lazarus was remembering your voice
When you called him from the grave.

If you brought him back to life from death,
Could you not live after your last breath?

Three days later, it wasn't long,
Lazarus joined the believers' throng.

Christ was risen, redemption complete.
Life won over death; the victory, how sweet!

## Peter—Hope Never Dies  (John 21:15-17)

From the moment the rooster crowed,
The sifting began.
His Lord he declared he'd die for,
But he was just a man.

Somewhere between tears of sorrow
And dining with his risen Lord on the shore,
Peter may have remembered walking on the water,
And hope entered his heart's door.

"Do you love me?"
Jesus did three times repeat.
From Peter's soul the answers poured.
"Lord, you know I love you."

"Feed my sheep," was Jesus's command
Three times over as they walked on the sand.

From Christ's mandate to Peter to feed his sheep
Came three thousand souls saved; a harvest was reaped!

If Peter could begin his ministry anew,
Dear precious readers, we can too.

## How Like You    (John 4:25-26)


Don't lose heart
Over mistakes wrought.

Remember the woman at the well?
The bad choices she made,
The consequences she paid?
Years of consequences paid.

Then one day, Lord,
There you were,
Revealing yourself to her!
How like you.

## Parable of the Ten Virgins  (Matthew 25:1-13)


Oh, to be wise, to be ready
At the midnight cry
To go out to meet him
When the bridegroom comes nigh.

With wicks in our lamps trimmed
And oil in our vessels full to the brim,
We can enter into the marriage with him.

Not so for the foolish with empty vessels,
Out buying oil,
Returning to a shut door,
Their futures forever spoiled.

Let us be as the wise virgins
Who have counted the cost,
And not the foolish ones,
Paying for their loss.

Everyday People in an Everyday World

## Is More Enough? (1 Timothy 6:6)


Oh, what a pretty dress!
And look at that cute hat.
Aren't these shoes just darling?
Hey, I can have them all today.
How about that?

All it takes is a plastic card
Or even a traveler's check.
"Don't leave home without one."
Ah, now I'm picturing a brand-new deck.

What's next on my list?
Let's see, there are so many choices.
"Buy me, buy me, don't wait,"
Shout many voices.

Shopping is fun! Had a pretty good day.
Thank goodness I didn't have to pay right away.

Would you look at all these bills?
They seem to have come so soon.
It kind of takes away from the thrill.
Maybe that dress wasn't so over the moon.

Payday has come for all that stuff.
And the truth is
More will never be enough.

# Going for the Gold   (1 Timothy 6:17)


What do you want?
What do you need?
Are you going for the gold?
Stop and consider; take heed.

How many hours of your day
Are you giving to work?
How many are left to play?
Or time with your loved ones
Who wait patiently, come what may?

How big is your deal?
How high is the cost?
Is it worth the price
If your family feels loss—

The loss of your presence
From day to day,
From choices you made
To do things your way?

Won't you listen to their cries,
Listen to their pleas?
Come join them in living life.
You won't have regrets; you'll see!

*9*

# Heaven

---

**Oh, the Glory**   (Isaiah 33:17)

Life will have seemed a moment
When at last I see your face.
Oh, the glory at the end of the race!

---

# Before I Go (Jesus to His Church)

(John 13:1; Psalm 145:4)

Before I go,
I want you to know
I love you so.

Before I leave
I ask you to believe,
Believe as long as you breathe.

Before I depart,
I give you my heart
To hold while we're apart.

And while I'm away,
Tell others of me
That they may see.

Before I go, let's share a smile
For we'll see each other in just a little while.

## Ties That Bind

You have to die to live—John 12:24.
You have to lose to find—Matthew 16:25.

A brand-new heart—Ezekiel 36:26.
A brand-new start—2 Corinthians 5:17.

These are the heavenly ties that bind.

## At Heaven's Door   (Psalm 16:11)

"Dear Lord," we sometimes say,
"Am I really worth waiting for?"

"Oh, yes, my child!
For you I cried in Gethsemane.
For you I died at Calvary.
For you I bore sin's penalty.
All for the joy of welcoming you home
At heaven's door!"

## Dying  (Revelation 4:1a)

When my body lies still
In the grave on a hill,
Do be aware
I am not there!

I've heard his voice
Like a trumpet blowing,
And find my real self going
To heaven!

I fly beyond a meteor's pace
On this last leg of the race, homeward!

And as I cross the finish line,
I see your smile returning mine.

## Heavenly Arrival (2 Corinthians 5:8)

As I arrive in heaven
I feel my heart will burst!

And here you are to greet me, Lord.
You wanted to be the first!

## The Last One   (Luke 15:7, 10)


Sometimes I wonder who will be the last one,
The last soul saved for time and eternity,

Coming to thee on bended knee,
Confessing sin and being set free
At the foot of Calvary's tree.

The last soul greeted by heaven's applause,
Redemption's plan is complete!

Now all your children are home safe
And walk on golden streets!

## Premise

While writing this book, there was a prompting to include the topic of hell. Though not a popular subject, it is a validated truth in God's Word.

Since it was deemed important to be addressed on numerous occasions by our Lord Jesus himself, I believe we need to acknowledge the reality of sin's ultimate consequence, which is eternity without God.

May this small section of poems inspire souls to take a step of faith to trust Christ for salvation and avoid consequences of eternity without hope, without him.

# And Then There Was Silence   (1 Samuel 2:9b)

Loud voices—
Boisterous, clamoring, defiant,
Abusive, angry, sarcastic, and foolish.

They cry, "Listen to me, listen to me!
I have something to say.
Don't talk; this is my time, this is my day!"

Is this the sound of your voice?
Sooner or later, you will leave this earth.
Your voice will be silent.

But there is a day coming
When you will have to say
Why you chose your way
Instead of his.

His ... the One who loved and died for you
To save your soul for eternity.

The first question will be,
"Is your name in the Lamb's Book of Life?"

Now he has your attention.
Now you are listening breathlessly to hear your name.
It is not found.

Now you have to depart
And go to the abode of the second death.

You hear voices, weeping, and wailing.
You realize your own voice
Is the one you hear above the others.
And no one is listening to you.

Your greatest regret is that
While you were talking, talking, talking,
You missed your invitation for eternal life.

Such loss, not choosing the cross.
And now there is the silence of his voice, forever.

## Are You the Baddest of the Bad?
(Luke 16:19–26)


You think you're rough.
You think you're tough.
You think you're the baddest of the bad.

You fight to the end.
You refuse to bend.

Nothing can make you repent.
Not even God's Son, heaven sent.

You dig your heels in
And choose to sin until the end.

Then when you die come words truly spoken.
One second in hell, and you will be broken.

# 10

# Funerals

---

**How Still**   (Matthew 28:1-8)

How very still, how very quiet
Was the tomb where Jesus lay.
Until the third day!

---

## Stepping Out of the Grave (John 14:19)

Graves, graves everywhere.
Proof that all who live will die.

But,

Who is that stepping out of the grave?
It's Jesus, our conqueror, mighty to save.
And because the captain of our souls
Has prepared the way
We, too, will step out of the grave someday!

## Victory (1 Corinthians 15:51–57)

Dear Jesus,

A sacrifice that knows no bounds.
Triumph in your sacred wounds!

Joy unspeakable, oh, the sound.
Victory o'er the grave and tomb!

# Death Is but a Shadow

**(Psalm 90:10 (by Moses); Genesis 15:1)**

Death is but a shadow
To those who love you, Lord.
Nothing to fear, we hold you dear
And fly homeward to you,
Our exceedingly great reward!

## One Breath
## Away    (Matthew 25:21; 2 Thessalonians 2:1–2)

One breath away—
Is today the day?
Will I hear you say,
"Well done, thou good and faithful servant?"

Oh, God, I pray by my side stay.
When my last breath is taken
Let my faith not be shaken,
And I'll awaken with thee in eternity!

# *11*

# Witnessing

---

## Living Coal   (Isaiah 6:6–8)

Your grace is beyond description.
Its language is so fair.

Lord, place a live coal from the altar on my lips.
Enable me thy grace to share.
Oh, that I may dare!

---

## Hello (Isaiah 41:6)

Lord, who will you bring to me today as I go my way?
Whether out and about or home with chores,
Reveal to me your open doors.

A smile, a helping hand, a word
Can bring encouragement when heard.

So fill my heart today as to others you and I say,
"Hello!"

## Send Me  (Isaiah 6:8)

How restless the hearts, Lord,
That will not turn to you.
There is no peace or joy displayed
In all they say or do.

Hope is elusive,
Contentment hard to find.
The enemy of this world
Has deceived their hearts and minds.

Throughout the years,
With all their fears,
They trudge, unhappy souls.
Who will go and tell them
That you can make them whole?

Send me, God, send me.
Use me to help them see.
Give your words to pierce their heart
That your Spirit may impart
Words of life and victory over strife.

And blessed be the day when they can sing
Of victory that Jesus brings!

## Today, if You Hear His Voice (Hebrews 3:15)

"Today, if you will hear his voice,
Harden not your heart."
Eternity is a long, long time to be apart.

Apart from the One
Who gave his life
To save your soul
And make you whole.

Won't you answer his plea from Calvary?
When you hear his voice, you have a choice.
"Choose this day whom you will serve."

## Repent (Mark 1:14–15)

"Repent" is the invitation.
"Repent" is the fervent call.
"Repent" entreats the Savior.
"Come one, come all!"

## Was I Salt and Light? (Luke 12:12; Colossians 4:6)

How many have heard your Word
Because I spoke when my spirit awoke?

Did I follow through when prompted by you?
Was I salt and light before the night fell
On those who knew you not?

Oh, God, give grace that when I see you face-to-face
It can be said as I walked earth's pilgrim path,
"Well done my child, you spoke on my behalf."

## Fulfill the Call   (Proverbs 15:23)

Help me, Lord, to fulfill your call
And give with joy my all.

A word spoken in due season can make a heart sing.
It can lighten a load of care
And encourage others that you are always there.

Use me in your perfect plan
To bless one by one the hearts you have fanned.

## Thought for Today (John 3:16)

Help me to remember, Lord,
Today and every day,
That everyone I meet or see
Is someone you died for.

## Divine Appointments (Galatians 6:10)

Days, nights, years go by.
One by one, gone as a sigh.

How much time do we spend waiting
And miss opportunities by hesitating?

Divine appointments come one by one,
Entrusted to us from the Father and Son.

How precious these moments sent from above,
Bidding us to join these missions of love.

Let us make haste to do his will
That the courts of heaven may be filled!

## Awake! (Romans 13:11a)

Awake, awake!
This is no time to sleep.
Awake my soul.
It's time to reap.

# Benediction

There's room at the cross for you.
There's room at the cross for you.

Though millions have come,
There's still room for *one*.

Yes, there's room at the ✝
for *You.*

# About the Author

This composition of poetry by Faye Stewart was inspired by her strong Christian faith. These poems are brief enough to give the readers a moment of reflection and clarity on an element of faith. They can turn to scripture citations noted at the beginning of each poem, and by doing so, they can easily add the book to a daily devotional practice or find a moment of solace in their God in the middle of a hectic day.

Faye's first book of poetry is titled *The Road to the Cross Leads Home.* She is thankful to the Lord for granting her the opportunity to write a second volume of poems inviting readers to meet him at the cross.

She lives in Sandston, Virginia and is blessed by her sons, grandsons and grand-daughter, her sister, and dear friends— all gifts from God.

Printed in the United States
By Bookmasters